Who Am I-Our People, Our Land, Our History, Our Culture

Malcom Mcgee

BookLeaf Publishing

Presentation by *BookLeaf Publishing*

Web: www.bookleafpub.com

E-mail: info@bookleafpub.com

ISBN: 9789357445382

First edition 2021

DEDICATION

I dedicate this book to every African worldwide whether in America, Africa, the Islands or elsewhere.

Who Am I?

Who am I?
I am Marcus Garvey standing up for my race.
I am a truth teller like Malcolm X and Khalid right in their face.
I am a motivator to rise us up by economic, psychological and spiritual unity.
I am an organizer to revolutionize our minds to come together as a conscious family.
I am a helper-rising to love and understand my people.
I am a life changer to rise revolutionaries out of unconscious sheeple.

I am Patrice Lumumba who was trying to help his people achieve liberation but was murdered by the CIA.
I am my hood, my beautiful black people don't play.
I am the life of the hard knocks-built up stress and pain.
I am my ancestors-we endured the torture, humiliation, homicide, genocide and 400 years of pain.
I am freedom and liberation from the words that come out of my mouth and flow out of my pen.
I am RBG, Black Panthers, the BLA-they all run in my blood within.

I am Dr. Ben-writing books to elevate our minds.
I am Amari Baraka-poetry running in my veins; writing to poetically grind.

I am Dr. Angela Degruy and Dr. Na'im Akbar-teaching knowledge of black psychology and knowledge of self.
I am the reviver-taking those revolutionary books off of the dusty shelf.
I am the blood of the millions of my ancestors in the Native American wars, in the Trail of Tears, in the Native American and Afrikan genocide and slavery, on the slave ships, on the plantations.

I am black! I am Afrikan! I am God's greatest creation!

My Family

We are divine.
That was God's design.
Looking at the "Sun" of God, accepting my divinity.
Waking up in the morning to Mother Earth's protection and serenity.
Vibing to Oshun, Lauren Hill, Erykah Badu, Bone Thugs and India Arie.
Chilling with the fam talking about life, spitting bars and writing poetry.
This is the revolution, it may not be shown on tv.
Instead, they show us killing each other and us going to jail, but no unity.
Weed smoke in the air, chakras up, pouring libations.
Talking about eating healthy, while using poetry and rap to heal the world and educate this fucked up generation.

We gotta get up and get this work done.
Stressing about grades but that college war has to be won.
My brotha Jordan about to go to UCF and Nemo about to go to FAMU.
No matter where we go, ain't nothing going to break up the crew.
My first PEACE club meeting, I met these two.
Overtime I got to know Alisha, Rodnika and everyone else too.
Real recognize real.

I knew I was where I needed to be from the vibes I felt, and people I met; it's time to link up, think, spit poetry and chill.

I got my whole mothafucking family.
UF and Santa Fe linking up, we are the essence of universality.
We're 10-15 deep, PEACE Club, Black On Black Rhyme-DopenMic.
Cyphers every 15 minutes, we're coming like a bomb strike.
Me and Desirae go way back, back to DUVALLL!!!
Kaleidoscope got Dopenmic running Gainesville, now watch her ball.
Dj Olympus on the turntables and that music blasting;
I'm looking forward to knowing him better.
I got all of this music and vinyl, it's time to get my record player.
Calling each other up talking about open mic.
Rolling up in the joint day and night.
Fists in the air while using our Nubian minds.
Our words creating change within people to heal the dumb, deaf and blind.
I give thanks to my poetry family in Jacksonville, who built me up to who I am today.
Ms. Tonya, Ebony, Neal, Dwight, Cheryl, Nica, The IGive, Ahynte-my respects, I have to pay.
All Power to the People, All power to the poets of this nation.
All power to my family, I love y'all is the situation.

Who We Are-What We Are

Black people, we are Afrikan.
African American people, we are Afrikan.
Jamaican people, we are Afrikan.
Haitian people, we are Afrikan.
We are Afrikans in the Bahamas and the Caribbean.
We are Afrikans in London.
We are Afrikans in Barbados.
We are Afrikans in Trinidad and Tobago.

We are Afrikans in Western Sahara.
We are Afrikans in Morocco.
We are Afrikans in Algeria.
We are Afrikans in Tunisia.
We are Afrikans in Lybia.
We are Afrikans in Egypt.
We are Afrikans in Mauritania.
We are Afrikans in Mali.
We are Afrikans in Niger.
We are Afrikans in Chad.

We are Afrikans in Sudan.
We are Afrikans in Eritrea.
We are Afrikans in Senegal.
We are Afrikans in Guinea-Bissau.
We are Afrikans in Gambia.

We are Afrikans in Guinea.
We are Afrikans in Sierra Leone.
We are Afrikans in Liberia.
We are Afrikans in Côte d'Ivoire.
We are Afrikans in Togo.

We are Afrikans in Ghana.
We are Afrikans in Nigeria.
We are Afrikans in Benin.
We are Afrikans in Cape Verde.
We are Afrikans in Cameroon.
We are Afrikans in Central African Republic.
We are Afrikans in South Sudan.
We are Afrikans in Djibouti.
We are Afrikans in Somalia.
We are Afrikans in Ethiopia.

We are Afrikans in Kenya.
We are Afrikans in Uganda.
We are Afrikans in Rwanda.
We are Afrikans in Burundi.
We are Afrikans in Democratic Republic of
Congo-Kinshasa.
We are Afrikans in Republic of Congo-brazzaville.
We are Afrikans in Gabon.
We are Afrikans in Equatorial Guinea.
We are Afrikans in São Tomé and Principe.
We are Afrikans in Tanzania.

We are Afrikans in Seychelles.
We are Afrikans in Angola.
We are Afrikans in Zambia.

We are Afrikans in Malawi.
We are Afrikans in Mozambique.
We are Afrikans in Madagascar.
We are Afrikans in Zimbabwe.
We are Afrikans in Botswana.
We are Afrikans in Namibia.
We are Afrikans in Comoros.

We are Afrikans in Lesotho.
We are Afrikans in South Africa.
We are Afrikans in Burkina Faso.
We are Afrikans in Swaziland.
We are Afrikans in Mauritius.
We are Afrikans in Réunion.
We are Afrikans around the world.

Drop your American mentality and find your true roots.
See the truth that lies within you.
The truth that they have tainted, painted over, walked over and ignored that is in all of us.
We are Afrikan and Afrikans must rise.
It is time for us to stand up and survive.
It is within our souls and minds.
It is what flows through our veins, it is what we all must find.
We must not be blind anymore, we must find what they are hiding.

UNITY!
TRUST!
REVOLUTION!

UPLIFTING OF RACE!
UPLIFT CULTURE!
REPAIR MOTHER AFRIKA!
ACCEPT THAT WE ARE AFRIKANS!
STAND UP AS ONE!
FIGHT AS ONE!
CHANGE AS ONE!
THINK AS ONE!
LOVE AS ONE!
FIGHT AS ONE ARMY!
PROTECT AS ONE NATION!
UPLIFT AND NURTURE AS ONE VILLAGE!
We are the…
UNITED NATION of AFRIKA!
No one can tell us who we are not.
No one can tell us what we cannot do.
No one can tell us what we can't achieve.
No one can dictate our future.

No one can force us to do or say anything because…
WE ARE ONE!
ONE AFRIKA!
ONE PEOPLE!
ONE RACE!
ONE MIND!
ONE HEART!
ONE SOUL!

We will rise.
We are not states.
We are not countries.
We are not nations.

We are…
ONE NATION!
We will be heard.
We will be seen.
We will make change.

Finding My Identity

When I feel the great sun on my skin, I know I am
purified, washed away from my sins.
I go down to the river to wash when they say that black
is a curse.
I find myself breaking mirrors trying to get rid of the
darkened thirst.
A plague to myself and a curse and threat to America.
As they raise the American flag and tell me to go back to
Africa.
The preacher said to bathe in the river and be baptized.
Study the bible and pray and my soul will be revitalized.
They said the others have Drapetomania- a mental
illness disease.
I hear the elder singing about freedom then gagged and
dragged by her knees.

There are people telling me to be proud of my race and
being black.
While I see police officers putting 15 bullets in our back.
While the court system locks him up for 20 years for
trying to survive.
While the little girl is left alone, struggling desperately
to stay alive.
While everyone I know is hooked on government
pumped drugs.
I see my brothas killing our own-massas street puppets
while they call themselves thugs.

I see massa bucks coming down the street to see how many women they can impregnate.
I see my sistas saying that they don't need us-generational black hate.
I see they shoot us down like animals unarmed while flying their flag so high.
Unless it's within their system with their corporate America ladder, they won't let us rise even if we wanted to try.

Trap houses, corner stores and liquor stores owned by Jewish and Asians are all through my hood.
I see my family going away just for trying to do good.
Unhealthy fast food places while they take all the holistic health stores.
Watered down European lies lead us to their open prison doors.
Feds and police raids with their slave catcher dogs to hunt us down.
Dragging us to their human zoos in small metal cages or shooting us dead to the ground.
Masking reality by claiming racism doesn't exist.
But getting mad and punishing me for loving myself, saying black power, preaching unity and raising my fist.
If we just stay obedient and docile slaves, then we are free in their eyes.
But if we try to rebel against the system, they feed us more pseudoscience and lies.
The hood is a breeding plantation for pain, poverty, death and exploitation.
Running towards freedom for over 400 years and still stuck on the plantation.

Realizing that this isn't a game, its set up for me to lose and they don't want me to win.
I give up, blame it on my blackness and follow them to wash away my sins.
I bow down to the white Jesus Christ as they tell me that it is the will of God that I am in bondage.
God made this black beast by mistake.
I had to be civilized-kill the beast for a man to make.

Brainwashing me as they control me through fear.
They say that they can make a man out of me but the negative names they call me is all I hear.
They show me the court to prison system.
They show me how quick they can kill one of my own when we rebel and don't listen to them.

Brainwashing me through money.
Fighting to survive-I become a slave to their job, their money, and a corporate America monkey.
Waiting for that minimum wage check to hit my bank.
Living paycheck to paycheck; barely surviving as my brain goes blank.
Eating rice, butter and cereal for breakfast, lunch and dinner.
Losing my money on scratch off tickets and the lotto hoping that I'm the next winner.
Mortgage three months late, food stamps got cut off, they just cut the electricity.
While they claim that they're struggling-this is real struggling and poverty.

Brainwashing me through school.
A restricted white-washed, indoctrinated, European based, systematic brainwashing, corporate-controlled education system to make me a fool.
Math only helps my cousin count his drug money.
Having no idea about our empires, our contributions and our royalty.
Teaching me nothing of my real history.
Made up stories of Columbus found the world, Africa is a primitive continent with apes and trees-my ancestors are all a mystery.
Black people were just slaves, Natives were savages and everything was all and well.
Fattening me up with the lies that they sell.

Brainwashing me from the corrupt music industry.
Selling us negative images, stereotypes and negative names of black/Afrikan people to snuff out all and any hope and positivity.
Any conscious singers and rappers who rap about a positive message won't be allowed on the radio and will be dealt with accordingly.
I will be a wierdo and an outcast if I don't listen to music of today's popular culture.
Anything about uplifting, uniting black women and men, they send reinforcements to pick you like vultures.
Sex, money and drugs sells so that is what we should endorse and promote.
I try to write about my struggle and improving it, but when I get in the booth, my words are shoved back down my throat.

Brainwashing me through politics.
Telling me to vote either democrat or republican or this nation will burn in tyranny but forgetting to tell me that it's just a pile of tricks.
The voting polls are full but the president does nothing to improve the conditions of my race.
Am I voting for a dirty, money-power hungry politician or a man with a black face?

Trying to find myself under all of the white while trying to hide the dark.
An old man was sitting by me riding the bus and told me to accept and embrace the blackness-that's a start.
How when I was taught that being black is a sin, a curse, a crime?
We die, go to prison and can't get anywhere-our lives are nightmares not a nursery rhyme.
He told me to open my mind, unlearn everything I've learned and find the truth in the lies.
I listened more and more to the old church songs-the struggle, the screams, the cries.
I found peace within them as I struggled with my identity.
The more I listened, the more people I ran into as if talking with the elders was my destiny.
The elders were talking, singing me slave stories; I listened to the ones with Drapetomania.
Giving me wisdom, history, riddles, names-Assata, Newton, Sankara, Toure', Nkrumah, Mumia.
They told me to read, analyze, think and understand.

John Henrik Clarke, Dr Yosef Ben, Dr. Joy DeGruy,
Chancellor Williams are some of the scholars of our
black land.
They told me to look deeper, in between the lines-but
Malcolm X was a terrorist and who is Marcus Garvey?
Allow the ancestors to teach you your history.
Where is Egypt, isn't Africa full of booty scratching
monkeys, what Black Wall Street?
Allow your mind to freely flow, research, learn to break
your chains.
The more you find, the more you will be in pain.
The more knowledge you know, the more you become a
threat.
Right now, you are their greatest asset.
Learn your power, your worth, don't just run away-burn
the plantation.
The sun of God hits your skin every day to remind you
of God's greatest creation.
Listen to everything, think, research and learn.
Give in to that inner voice telling you to go, run the other
way, rebel and turn.
Allow Olorun to speak through you-He will open your
eyes.
What? Who is that?
He is the great spirit from which you feel from the sun in
the skies.
Today-the great Muhamad Ali died-he did way more
than just boxing for our history.
There are many more things in life than being afraid to
do anything because they will shut you up-you will see.
The great Afeni Shakur died, but all you heard about was
Prince.

Look up COINTELPRO-the black community has
barely been able to recover since.
I've lived though many things, I'm only 73.
The black skin is who you are-you will figure it out-your
only 20-you can only find your future through your
history.
Be patient with yourself and your people-you won't
understand everything-you have to take it slow.
Knowledge, wisdom and understanding is the only way
you will learn and grow.
Read, communicate with your ancestors and elders.
Listen to the wind, look to the trees.
Feel the sun nourishing your skin-Mother earth will
show you what you need to see.
Scrub off your white face and listen to the pain, love,
history etched into your beautiful black skin.

Find yourself-stop letting them exploit and manipulate
you within.
Find your purpose, find your ancestors and you will
eventually find your people.

I Am Who They Are-Our History and Struggle Will Live On (My Goodbye Letter)

I am my ancestors, their blood runs in my veins.
Their struggle is my struggle, I can still feel their pains.
I have inherited my emotions from my ancestor's and their past.
The rage kicks in from the genes of ancestors, the Afrikan outcast.
We started from the top, now we're here.
Stripped from our African King and Queenship to live in European domination and fear.

The modern day Emmitt Till.
The new age slavery, the legal way to murder and kill.
The chains on my feet and the whips on my back.
The systematic oppression; being shot, killed and locked up just for being black.
The stolen history to be replaced with lies.
The lynched bodies to quiet the cries.
The torture of helplessly watching them beat and gang-rape my sister.

Cops killing my cousins while shouting “go back to Africa nigger”.
Don’t whistle to that white girl or she will claim “rape!”
“Let’s lock that animal up into constitutional slavery, he’s a disobedient ape.”
Don’t look that white boy in the eyes, you’re a rebellious and non-submissive slave.
Call the police and let them beat him to show him how to behave.
He has a great resume and graduated from UF but he’s black.
“He might bring drugs, thugs and guns into my company, let put his resume at the bottom of the stack”

The Europeanized and corrupt system that isn’t going to do shit.
It’s time to show them instead of just shouting “don’t forget.”
George Zimmerman and Darren Wilson killed one of us but they’re walking around signing autographs.
We sit and whisper “no justice-no peace-never forget” while standing in line to buy an I-Phone 5 from the oppressor; while they hysterically laugh.
It’s time to live "never forget" from the end of the master’s whip.
I feel my ancestors’ battle cry, it’s time to take the streets back until my blood drips.
Let Malcolm X rise from his grave.
It’s time to stop marching and start stomping until their surrender flag is waved.
Willie Lynch is on his way to put us back in place.

Mr. Lynch is coming, it's time to rise up and show my face.
I tried to keep quiet, but my ancestors wouldn't let me.
My ancestors' blood beats through my heart while they scream in my ears to rise, fight, create change and write poetry.
Intelligent black man, I'm seen as a threat.
They label me a terrorist to legalize my killing; that's how the system is set.

Fuck the government, fuck the police, fuck the Justice system.
Fuck the law; the law that they are the divine rulers and they are God.
It's time to stand up to the "What else do you want? Your president is black."
He has death threats knocking at his door and we have ten targets on our back.
They might lynch me before my poetry goes viral but my ancestors' won't go down without a fight.
I will die shouting to our Afrikan Kings and Queens until reality comes into sight.
Look at the streets painted with our blood, look at the trees that drip our blood; our struggle and our pain.
The living trees filled with the angry souls of our ancestors, our history, and our Afrikan name.
I let them free to come fight with me; learning from their expertise and experience.

I'm not scared to die; I know that they are coming to kill me, I just pray they kill me fast.

They will try to shut me up in any way, but my poetry,
my fight, my soul and my message will last.
My great grandfathers' legacy will live on through
others because they can never stop the flow of our
Afrikan blood.
Our history, our emotions, our struggle will keep flowing
when my body hits the street with a thud.
I might be thrown in Solitary Confinement, Maximum
Security Prison just to be put on death row.
They will try to shut us up, keep us in submission but
you must be ready to stand up and shout.
Stand with all of your heart and mind because they prey
on the weak, smell fear and doubt.

As bullets fly into my body, just remember the truth,
keep the fight and teach our real history.
My soul will be waiting in the trees for someone else to
stand up and fight; hoping that my poetry won't become
a mystery.
Be not afraid of evil, for darkness is among us but the
Afrikan Nation shall survive!

The Hanging Tree of Truth and Reality

Are you coming to the hanging tree?
Strange fruit hangs down for you and me.
We still see the ropes that hang.
Remembering the scars from the whips; the sounds and cries that rang.
Our families and ancestors whisper to us to run as fast as we can to freedom and safety.
We run and 400 years later, still stuck in slavery.
As we run, the midnight moon sets in.
I heard the dead man sing and felt a strange sickening feeling within.
The singing turned into cries and screams.
The earth below my feet started moving.
As I neared the tree, the roots took a hold of my feet.
The screams turned into whispers-some saying to keep going and others telling me to stop before death meets.
I keep going and touch the tree.

The delicate flesh being whipped to shreds.
The mother crying after being raped in that bed.
The child screaming for her mother while being stripped away from her family.
I hear voices telling me to let go of the tree.
I try to break my trance but the roots grip my feet and the trunk pulls my hand in deeper.

Images of dogs attacking our bodies.
Burning flesh, death, pain and scary memories.
The sounds of chains being dragged across the ground.
A teenage boy running away and being chased by hounds.
Bombs and fires with crosses from the Ku Klux Klan.
Death of our people, destroying our cities and land.
Treaties broken and the trail of Tears.
Naked women lined up in shackles as they are thrown into the rivers.

Crying, fighting, I don't know what to do.
Tree… tree let me go, but it wasn't through.
I hear spirits singing-Are you coming to the hanging tree?
To understand your history.
Your life is a mystery.
So let me show reality.
Blackness approaches but I'm forced to open my eyes.
They lit the man on fire, blood curdling cries.
Cross burning in the background as they light his house on fire.
Dragging another frail body through the hood as the smoke rise higher.

Waking up to bombs blasting through the air.
1921-Tulsa Oklahoma bombing of our city like they don't care.
Little airplanes with bombs-to them, this is what peace is.
My little Africa blown to pieces.

Running, terrified, Nooo, I screamed as my uncle's store went up in flames.
America is corrupt and the KKK states that Natives and Africans are to blame.
Crying and scared, I look for safety.
Destruction everywhere, body parts burned, my Afrikan family.
Help, Help, I scream but they just stand at the edge of the city and look.
Years later after they dumped my family in the river like trash, they hid it in the "history" books.

I'm shifted off into a small town.
Bloody and crying, I ask where I am from the people around.
Are you lost, the woman asked, you're in Florida, Rosewood-1923.
Noo, I don't want to see anymore, why are you showing the destruction of my family.
As I was walking, I heard the rumor that that white woman was raped.
Within a day, a white mob came, I wish we all could've escaped.
They lynched Mr. Carter right in front of my eyes.
They tortured my elder and laughed as all we could do was run away and cry.
They shot and killed Ms. Sarah, Mr. Sylvester, please don't go out on that porch.
The next day, he showed up dead and we woke up to his house being torched.
I stood there looking at the pain, one of the elders grabbed me and screamed run.

I couldn't believe it was happening again as they slaughtered our animals, killed our family and burned our houses for fun.
Mr. John Bryce rushed us onto his train to evacuate.
Gainesville FL bound, never to see my friends and family again, I just hoped they escaped.

Are you coming to the tree?
The only way you will be free.
Ax handle Saturday.
Showing you the truth today.

We were just sitting in the restaurant in 1960.
Niggers can't be here they said as they pointed to the "whites only" sign, see.
We were all tired, we just wanted equality.
We didn't come to fight; we don't want any hate.
The crowd got bigger as a white mob came ready to retaliate.
I got scared, sitting in the middle of downtown Jacksonville.
I looked around as things started escalating and the air stood still.
Calling us niggers, animals, darkies, they held ax handles and baseball bats.
They spit on us, and started beating us as we sat.
I thought, Mr. Hurst, please get me out of here.
We looked everywhere for cover as we ran in fear.
They chased us outside through streets while the cops stood idly by.

Then I woke up; the wind is here.

Blood puddles are everywhere.
Gun in hand.
I cannot understand.
Looking down, trying to make out his name.
Realizing that this isn't a game.
Sirens, the cops-pigs.
Knowing that if I retaliate, I will die because the game is rigged.
Concrete walls become my company.
My four best friends-the only thing that shelters me.
Follow the law, pull up your pants, speak proper English, go to school.
I want to listen to my ancestors but American society says that is not cool.
I look around in my freedome.
Realizing that I'm not safe in my own home.
4 shots, 16 shots, -in the blink of my eyes.
I watch my mother fall to the ground as they laugh and say nigger die.
The cameras were watching
But the so called Justice system does nothing
She abided by the law; what did she do wrong?
Just being black and people wonder why we can't get along.

I wake up to what I think is a nightmare.
Look out the window and stare.
News channels flickering.
As Democrips and Rebloodicans are bickering.
If he had only pulled up his pants, if they had only obeyed the law, if he had only listened to the cop.

My mother listening to the tel-lie-vision while they try to
justify why another body just dropped.
They had marijuana, he was resisting, what about black
on black crime.

Looking at my three-year-old brother who doesn't know
what being black means, I cry.
Knowing that I won't be able to protect him from reality
no matter how hard I try.
My mother says we need to get on our knees and pray.
But we've been praying for over 400 years, white cracka
Jesus ain't coming today.
I walk down the street and lay in a puddle of blood
where my brotha was slain last night.
The concrete sucks me in and I let it consume me
without a fight.
My skin is ripped off of me to expose my flesh.
I smell something burning, rotten, nothing fresh.
I felt like I couldn't breath as I desperately opened my
eyes.
Immense pain, then I realized.
As they tightened the noose around my neck, they said
that I was a terrorist and I was the one to blame.
For telling the truth, showing reality, creating change,
promoting unity.

Are you coming to the hanging tree?
Where they will bury all of our history.
Watch as they come to kill and lynch me.
To keep the truth a mystery.
They don't like I tell reality.

Trying to make us live in fantasy.
There's still hope for love and unity.
But it first starts with you and me.

OPEN YOUR EYES AND TOUCH THE TREE!

Our Mother is Their Targeted Victim

They raped our mother; Mother Afrika.
They call her the black America.
They penetrated her dark flesh with their white semen.
Impregnating her with Europeans.
They slapped her onto the floor, while they shouted that they are daddy.
Leaving scars on her as we screamed, "Stop hurting our mommy!"
They wrapped their arms around us and whispered in our ears "you are not the victims".
They forcefully thrust open her legs and stole the precious life that she was trying to hide from them.

Our mothers' cries and screams turned into melodies drifting through the air.
As they stripped us away and left her naked, dying and bare.
They invaded her pure vagina just to fuck her and leave.
Their erect penis abused her insides, feeding her lies for her to believe.
They didn't want to learn her intellectually.
They just came to dry her rich juices out sexually.
They came back for more with their neighbors to run threesomes while calling her a slut.
Denying the fact that they were the filthy pigs and mutts.

They tried to repair pieces of her tortured soul by
bringing back some of her children to Liberia and Sierra
Leone.
Europeanized countries formed by Britain and the
American Colonization Society so they can claim that
we were back home.
Not knowing where the scars came from because so
many hands have traveled up and down her delicate
flesh.
Deep wounds years old and scars that are fresh.
Her scabs started breeding infections.
With the loss of blood, her body started to malfunction.

They killed our mother; Mother Afrika.
They call her the backwards America.
They cut her veins to let her blood splatter on the floor.
Sending pieces of her tormented heart to all of her
children's door.
They lynched her and left her as a plaque on a tree.
Exploitation of her body and her people for free.

They changed her history and her name.
Our mothers' real name was Alkebulan: Arabic for "The
Land of The Blacks" " but the Romans got the acclaim.
The Kemmiu-ancient Egyptians described her with
"Af-Rui-Ka.
The Romans just Latinized this word to 'Africa'.
When Publius Scipio destroyed Carthage–a city-state in
northern Afrika, he added the last name-Africanus.

They claim a man from Spain called Leo Africanus said
her name was from the Greeks.
They didn't want to tell us that Ham; the youngest son of
Noah is our father, our real daddy.
The four Sons of Ham: Mizraim (Egypt), Cush (Sudan,
Ethiopia), Put (Lybia) and Canaan were our first family.

They tortured her body and her soul until she finally
collapsed.
We were selling our own families, now we were trapped.
They broke her down so we, her children couldn't
depend on her socio-economic muscle.
They took us, transporting us to the rest of the world to
force us to struggle.
Disorienting our identity and self-worth, then called our
mother the Dark Continent.
They took control of us, her people, her resources and
her environment.
They sold guns to our neighbors, making us fight,
enslave and kill for power.
Manipulating our minds to make us sell our own as
slaves every hour.

They taught us to kill, capture and compete against each
other.
The Portuguese manipulated our minds to take over our
mother.
They were attracted to our mother because of the gold on
her skin.
Exploitation and assimilation to deprive her of her
resources within.
They used her grave as a urinal.

They laughed and tried to burn her dead corps at her own
funeral.

AIDS, Ebola and SARS are laboratory-manufactured
viruses to control or mother land.
They put our mother on their lab table for diseases and
laughed as they held the cures in their hands.
They screamed in our ears that HIV originated in
chimpanzees in West Afrika, and that it mutated when
we hunted them for meat.
What was the Special Virus Cancer Program, who was
Dr. Gallo and who was giving our mother viruses like
treats?
Why did Dr. Gallo patent AIDS if it wasn't created?
They wanted her to die off quickly, so they injected it in
her warm veins and waited.

Fragments of our Afrikan society can be found hiding
beneath the destruction.
From her eulogy to resuscitation...
We, her children will revive our mother because we are
the Afrikan Nation.
There needs to be an Afrikan revolution.
There will be an Afrikan revolution.
Our mother, Mother Afrika will rise from being their
rape victim.
She will rise from their lynch ropes and take her life
back from them.
Our mother will rise.
We, her people will survive.

Melanin High

Prison cells are golden gates.
Living in earthly hell as our mental state.
Spitting bars to create more cages.
Dr Jekyll and Mr Hyde as we switch our faces.
Trying to hide our inner demons by conforming to society.
Brainwashed zombies of whitewashed American fantasy.
Chilling on the block, sitting in our chains.
While running away from freedom pains.
Homeboys playing executioner with our guns.
The executioner comes and we run.
Trying to find a way to survive without change.
Blame game-tag, you're it-claiming this is how life is arranged.
Waiting to get out of the hood.
Forgetting that concrete flowers can still be good.
Rising from the jungles of nightmares to be a shining star.
Being black and proud as we rise up and tell them who we are.
Trying to breathe, waiting to exhale.
Institutions set up, choking us to the ground to fail.
Man eat man-waiting to devour.
The animal in man as the hood turns sour.
Giving up our minds to the wolf for the slaughter.
Being fed lies, hearing faint laughs as they caught her.
Minds are garbage dumps through music and tv.

Running backwards while embracing the negativity.
Sucking us into black holes of fantasy.
Scrubbing the scars off of our backs-slowly forgetting our history.

Suffering from pride, ego, low self-esteem and confusion of self-identity.
No knowledge of self, as they say that we are free.
Controlled by cognitive dissonance, Stockholm syndrome and rejecting drapetomania.
Claiming that there's no more racism because this is the new millennia.
Grabbing the broom to brush the present and the past under the rug.
Kicking me off the porch when I pull and tug.
Playing a game called finding nemo-no finding dory.
Seeing others become conscious but forgetting the entire story.
Claiming being conscious and woke but still doing what massa tells them to do.
While still believing the media, the statistics, the pseudoscience and being lied to.
Grave yards of religious folk that claim we need the holy ghost.
Killing ourselves to be the next holy host.
Possessed by demons of materialism, our lives are seen through money.
The sheep laugh as my pontifications of unity are funny.
Rising out of that negative energy to find my own light.
They told me to pray but I would rather fight.

The darkness of my universe is glittered by stars.

Every five pointed bright light on this black skin is a historical scar.
Reminding me of my ancestors struggle and pain.
Telling me my purpose through the blood in my veins.
Teach, heal and unify.
No one will be able to take us down even if they try.
Universally fortified.
Melanin satisfied.
9 ether, Third eye open.
So much knowledge, the lid is broken.
A walking contradiction.
Black dark chocolate addiction.
Black God thesis.
Mind over matter-got that psychokinesis.

I am God in flesh-dust of the land.
Stardust magic-you can't even understand.
Defying gravity; extensions of my soul.
Getting dreadlocks was my essential goal.
Throwing crowns on all of my sistas heads.
Waking up my brothas from their death beds.
Pineal gland cleansing-walking like Kings and Queens.
Accepting our divinity as light and energy sun beings.
Started from the top, now we here; it's time to go back up.
Ain't no started from the bottom, we woke up.
Descending from the heavens-Gods and Goddesses.
Waiting to sit on our throne and take back our palaces.
Flowing through existence, masters of our own universe.
666 mathematics of carbon-spitting crazy knowledge, people calling in the nurse.

My positive energy too high for this mic.
Knowledge overload for these speakers, Future and Fetty
Wap said this was my last strike.
Let me play you some Dead Prez and some Sa-Roc.
Got the heads moving to that lyrical therapy on the entire
block.
Conscious Plat, Oshun and Aisha Sekhmet.
Listening to that real knowledge-got rap stars
reevaluating the alphabet.

Writing this poetry like a dope fiend.
Rocking this shit out with that Red Black and Green.
My frequency's' on another level with the ankh on my
chest.
Listening to the elders and let the ancestors do the rest.
Rejecting the white Jesus-only deal with Maat and
Olorun.
Meditating and remediating through Mother Earth and
my ancestors, so clear the room.
Let me give you this knowledge through this poetry.
Got them books in my hand, Malcolm X and Marcus
Garvey.
Dr. Ben, Na'im Akbar, Thomas Sankara, Kwame
Nkrumah, Patrice Lumumba, Gaddafi, Mugabe, Stokely
Carmichael, MLK, Dr. John Henrik, Muhammad Ali,
Assata Shakur, Huey P. Newton, Harriet Tubman, Nat
Turner-the real OG's.
I'm done with this shit, I'm out-now who with me?

Black Woman-Black, Beautiful God

Black Woman.
You are strong.
Don't believe the hype of the world, they are wrong.
You don't need to go to the gym to be skinny and short and that's it.
You don't need to eat more and work out to be thick.
You don't need skin lightening cream.
At night, I hear your cries and screams.
You're not light enough so you're not beautiful.
You're too light so you're not suitable.
They don't like natural hair so you need weave.
If you don't have long hair and makeup, then he will leave.

You are beautiful however you are.
Those stretch marks are your battle scars.
You hold the universe in your vagina and every continent on your delicate skin.
Black woman, being black is not a sin!
When someone touches you, they touch every country and continent on earth.
You are the alpha and omega, first and last from the start to the end of our birth.
Your skin glistens in the sun as you accept your divinity.
Put on that crown, you are a Queen and let all see.

The night envelops your body at night.
Your black body is the essence of milk chocolate dipped in gold; it is your birthright.
Melanin so rich because of the gold on your skin.
People will try to exploit you to steal your gold within.
When you open your legs, you give a piece of the world away.
A world that you created from the beginning of time and day.
They call you bitch and hoe.
Because they want to take your resources then blame you for your baggage and cargo.
Put down that perm and make up and learn who and what you are.
You are the entire universe, you are the biggest and brightest star.
You are a sister, a Queen.
You are the birth of the nation, the beginning of everything.
You are crafted from the dark and rich soils of Africa.
Don't ever allow people to brand your beauty from the European standards of America.
They are selling your melanin for $300 a gram, getting lip, breast and butt injections.
Trying to mimic your hairstyles and physical features but when you come out naturally, you are a rejection.
Black woman, you are due for extermination.
But no one can ever kill you because you are the essence of all creation.

Society tries to place certain limits on you and crunch you in a marginalized box.

They only portray negative images of you and claim you
are ugly but tell them to kick rocks.
The world doesn't appreciate your hard work of birthing
us and raising up men and women to become Kings and
Queens throughout the years.
We don't understand the hard work, blood, sweat and
tears.
Black woman, the things you have to see and endure.
Having to watch your sons grow up and die before they
reach 21.
Seeing your daughter get heartbroken or lose her
virginity because the boy thought it was fun.
Having to watch your creations destruct around you.
Praying, watching, crying.
While the world around you is dying.
400 plus years of rape and slavery-the pain and wounds
are still there because it never gets old.
Your children being stolen from you and sold.
Your husbands being beaten, bull whipped, and hanged.
Knowing that another one of your sons or daughters died
when you hear that gunshot that rang.
You were valued less than men and only used to breed.
They continued to find multiple ways to kill off your
seeds.
Tires burning, bullets flying but no one is there for you.
Bodies lying on the ground and another life that you
birthed is through.
You make sure that we eat, have clothes on our backs,
roofs over our heads.
While society runs over you and tells you that you don't
exist, you get up instead.

Black woman-stop falling in these traps that chain you up within.
Thinking that all you can be is a bad bitch because the emptiness you feel is only allowing you to feel like that within.
You think that showing your ass is the only way to get a man.
Sit back, relax, open up your mind and eyes and try to understand.
Self-esteem and self-love based off of how many followers and likes.
Slick boys use "Netflix and chill" to get them a bite.
Bite into what they think is a piece of meat.
Call the black woman bitches and thots when they can't eat.
Tell them, your body is not for consumption!

It's time to make love with your mind first and watch you go through a sexual eruption.
It's time to close your legs and see if these brothas can fuck your brain so hard, you're tired just spitting knowledge to each other.
Learning and understanding your divine spirituality because Earth is your mother.
Understanding real conversations.
Putting that phone down and working on higher vibrations.
Heaven and hell as your higher and lower ascension.
Growing out your natural hair as apart of your spiritual extension.
It's time to see if the brotha can lift you up so the "sun" of God can hit your skin.

Your gold glistening in the rays, feeling your love and protection within.
Reading the Autobiography of Assata Shakur, Afeni Shakur, watching Hidden colors 1,2,3, and 4.
Spitting knowledge at you from the Marcus Garvey book he just read as soon as you open the door.

I don't want y'all to give a piece of your body, I want y'all to feed our souls.
What are your ambitions, dreams, goals?
What are you going to do to make a change?
What are you going to do to improve the condition of our people?
What do you believe in, your spiritual systems and motivations?
How do you elevate your mind? What are your daily creations?
What do you feel is your purpose on earth, do you know?
If not, it's ok, we all have room to learn and grow.
What are your mistakes in life, how did it build you to be the person that you are to be?
I want you to be able to tell us more than just your favorite color and your relationship history.
I want you to learn how you grow, how you think and react.
Why do you do the things that you do, why do you feel those emotions, during a stressful situation, how do you act?
I want you to learn, understand and love yourself and learn true beauty.

Understand that cooking, cleaning and having sex is not
your duty.
Being a bitch, a hoe, a thot and giving it up whenever
men want to is not what God put you here for.
Taking care of the world alone without anyone by your
side to take care of you-no more.
The divine Creator-God created you for a higher purpose
than be mans and Amerikkan societies slave.

Black woman, it's time to break out of your chains.
Embrace your melanin and let your beauty reign.
Time to gain knowledge of self, love of self, acceptance
of self.
Time for rebuilding and elevation of self, respect of self.
Find your higher vibrations through discipline and
control of self.
Black woman, it's time to accept your God given Afrikan
divinity.
Allow the sun to nourish your skin and find inner peace,
love, and harmony.
Black woman you are beautiful, you are life, you are
black.
You must take your crown back.
It is time to command your existence; Black woman you
are God!

Empty Hosts of Death

Something else is there keeping us from healing.
Trying to see but blinded by the killing.
Eyes closed but trying to feel.
Nothing to grab as we are cooked for a meal.
Now we must see before it's too late.
Lead me out before the evil comes to take.
Is there anything else left in our soul?
Trying to define our very existence by our holes.
A dead corpse walking around.
Trying to pick up the pieces from the ground.
But everything we touch turns to ashes.
Trying to repair but we always crash.
Seeing the sun but it's too far to grab.
Wanting to believe that we are strong but our minds, we can't even have.

Becoming scared of the sun.
When it shines, we run.
Becoming roaches of society.
Running away from what's real while eating up their reality.
Empty hosts to be used.
Manipulated minds to be abused.
Hearts torn to shreds.
Souls are collected to keep us dead.
Getting prepared to catch the holy ghost.
Fighting to be another holy host.

Being raped and liking it as we look for more.
More things to choke us to sleep to drown out the screams behind the door.
Trying to kill the monster under our bed.
But watching the same scary movie over and over that we dread.
Hoping that if we watch it enough, we won't be scared but secretly praying for it to come.
Laughing as it eats us but screaming in fear.
Exploiting its sexual fantasies upon us as we let it near.

Being fed to the slaughter.
As we ignore the faint sounds of laughter.
The walking dead.
Trying not to relive the past but falling into the traps that we were fed.
Rising to see the same day over and over.
When will we cross over?
Day turns to night.
Vultures come to snuff out the light.
Picking out and eating our last little bit of sanity.
Creating an illusion that we live in-a fantasy.
Their venomous tongues lick our neck and roll down our back.
Guiding us to keep us on track.
The people of confusion.
Love creates our destruction.
Eyes and ears closed as we wait for the aliens to take over.
Death pervades through as the Passover.
Our walking corps is Satan's playground.
The hate unites us as we go round and round.

Getting higher and higher not realizing that we're really falling.

All doors open, all affected.
If we open our eyes and ears, we will see that it's all connected.
I'm struck down for telling reality.
Hung like a slave on the old oak tree.
They claimed it was all blasphemy.
Knowledge is all a mystery.
"Do not question anything, do what you're told."
Generations past, doing the same until you're old.
"Creativity is illegal, critical thinking is bad."
"Know the latest trends and follow the latest fad."
"Don't worry about anything else, you are protected and okay."
"Believe what we tell you and do as we say."
We are all sociopaths, mentally ill.
Homicide then suicide when there's no one else to kill.
Tag you're it, the blood bath grows.
The river that always flows.

I call upon the aliens to come save us from ourselves.
Find us from under the destruction that we've created within ourselves.
Find our souls even by means of extermination.
Spread the truth and reality to all the ends of the nation.
Unlock our minds from captivity.
End this horrible cycle of slavery.
Open our eyes or kill us all.
Wherever you are, from Mars or Jupiter.
We need you, you are our future.

No More Pawns and Puppets in the Babylon System

They say "We are the boss", we say "yes master".
"You will do whatever I tell you to do nigger."
"Now get down and pray that I don't get that whip."
We kneel before him and start to pray, but I pray that one day, the tables will flip.
"Now go fetch me a pail of water nigger."
I don't move, but my grin starts to get bigger.
"I know you heard me nigger", then he slap me in the face.
I get up, slap him back, "who you? You're a disgrace."

They are not boss anymore, we will rise in revenge.
We built this world; it's time to take it back, Afrika for Afrikans!
Marches and sit-ins don't work for us, we are the new generation.
Jim Crow laws and slavery don't control us; better find another way of segregation.
They couldn't keep us Afrikans down for too long, we've risen out of our graves.
They beg us not to go Nat Turner on them, we do more than that; we're done being slaves.

Revolutionizing with unity is our method, starting with infiltration.
I'm sorry Obama, but the White House is coming down tonight, our gift for our 500 years of our exploitation.

Rockefeller and Rothschild; just to name two.
Devils of this Sodom and Gomorrah; Europeans have gone wild and we are through.
They think that they are God, with this European Global Power Structure and racist system.
The European Jesus Christ or Julius Caesar, the description to fit them.
The plot to blow up the Twin Towers and money funneling to Al Qaeda to get our minds from reality.
The only way to talk with them is with guns and destruction; all they want is money.
Babylon will burn in the fire; it is too late to cry.
The devils, pigs and so called religious founders of this United States just lie.
Now gays and lesbians can walk down the aisle and say "I Do".
While dumbing us down, robbing us of reality and our Mother Afrika of her resources but this is nothing new.
Thieves of philosophy, resources and people from Afrika.
Wiping out our Natives to hide the truth of what they did to Native America.

It's time to check out the European plan:
"We hate you but we will give you free welfare and healthcare as long as you give your sons and daughters to me."

“Allow me to brainwash them to learn about Europeans and let them forget their history.”
“We hate you niggers but we will give you free AIDS and HIV tests.”
“As long as you give us your black men so we can lock them up in prison-constitutional slavery but you can have the rest.”
“We don’t want you niggers in our church but you may burn in the fires of hell, so here’s a book nigger.”
“You should read, study and live by this book and never question it, so I can get richer.”
“It is the will of God that you are in bondage; we are your God and you shall worship me.”
“Just give us your sons so we can control them in the school to prison pipeline and use them as pawns in the drug game on the streets so change cannot be.”
“We will send police officers into the hoods to go hunting and shoot any nigger animals in sight.”
“We will cover up the truth and call up our lawyer, judge and jury friends to make us seem right.”

“We will tell your nigger boys that they can’t be anything else in life except for street thugs, hustlers and ball players.”
“They eat it up; they treat their women like the bitches that they are as their mothers come to us, their white God in need of prayer.”
“We will tell your women that their bodies are the only thing that will get them through life.”
“They will shake their butts, glorify every man’s penis, have children that they can’t take care of and put themselves through strife.”

"We tell them that they won't be able to go to school if they have a child and they have to sell their bodies to try to take care of the household."

"We tell them that they have to drop out of school, let these thugs sleep with them, and then they are a true woman and are bold."

"While sleeping with every man, they get hooked on drugs, neglect and abuse their nigger children."

"They are mine then."

"Any nigger woman who tries to go to school, we will make sure tuition is very high; we will give them loans to mess up their credit."

"We will make it harder for them when they get that degree; single parents with a Master's Degree but can't even get a job at McDonalds. Making them start to regret it."

"We will allow you niggers to say "fuck the police" as long as you're our puppets and you have no control over your own life and mind,"

"Your men are our street army and we tell them to kill their own kind."

"We have control of your lungs as you smoke our marijuana and crack."

"We control your body as your men breed with women like our animals, and then leave you to never come back."

"Giving us more of your kind to manipulate, brainwash, exploit and use."

"If you retaliate in any way with these so called black liberation movements, we will just mass murder all of you because we have a short fuse."

"You don't have time to teach your children because you're too busy working for us, so just send your children to our schools."
"We will make sure that they won't know anything about themselves and their history."
"They all come from dirty, dumb slaves. African kings and queens, revolutionary movements, great African people in Africa and America will be a mystery."
"All they will see on T.V is the destruction of your race."
"Degradations of their women, their men only want money, sex and fame is blasted in their ears from the radio and T.V shows and news channels that throw it in their face."
"We will make sure they will think that their black skin is related to savage, slave and ghetto; they will want to be white."
"They will hate their skin, hate their people and believe anything that we say is right."

"We will raise them like a true human even though they will still be a nigger and an animal in our eyes."
"Feeding them false hopes of being accepted and fattening them up with lies."
"We will send them in the military to kill innocent people for our greed, to teach them how to be a good patriot and to build up their nation's pride."
"Make them think that they're fighting for their rights, in the name of democracy while our real intentions, we hide."

"Raising them up to be a so-called negro leader to teach that your kind needs to turn the other cheek and live in peace."
"We will tell them to tell you to suffer a little longer, make your children go to European school."

"Ask our white Gods who love us to help us become human because we are beasts".
"Please don't retaliate; they gave us free shelter (HUD, rent), free money (food stamps, TANF), free food (WIC, SNAP), free insurance (Medicaid) and a black president".
"We have these rights and these laws from our great constitution. They love us, isn't that evident?"
"The government was created from our perfect religious founding fathers and our issues are because of our own animalistic flaws."
"We just need to vote, go to school, read the bible, pray to our white God and submit and obey the laws."

Their plan to exploit, brainwash, Europeanize, kill and divide our Afrikan people and nation.
Destruction and eradication of our homes, communities, continent and our people is their creation.
Your Fourth of July.
Our Fourth of You Lie.
Your President's day.
Our Fuck the Law day.
Your Columbus day.
Our European Stupidity day.
Your Thanksgiving.
Our Thanks-killing.

Our Thank You Letter:

We thank you for lynching us, feeding us to sharks, cutting open our pregnant Afrikan Queens stomach with a machete, raping us, beating us with bull whips, the trail of tears, pulling our bodies apart with horses, stripping our lands, language, spirituality, history and culture away from us, colonizing us, keeping us in a systematic oppression, putting us in reservations, feeding our babies to sharks, tricking us, confusing and dividing us and stealing our precious resources from Mother Afrika.

We also thank you for European Global Power Structure, European teachings, stealing our culture and calling it yours, capitalism and imperialism, the Prison Industrial Complex and the "War on Drugs", Black Codes and Jim Crow laws, treating and hunting us like animals, breeding us, hiding our history and brainwashing us into loving America.

On Valentine's Day, we are going to show our love, thanks and appreciation.

For all of your hate, death, destruction, and exploitation.

As the White House is burned down.

The star spangled banner and the American flag is ripped in shreds, burning all over the ground.

The Department of Defense can't control us anymore; the death and destruction of our race runs in their veins.

The FBI keeps trying to arrest us on false charges with the cold death on their hearts, but we are done with these pains.

The CIA creates plans to murder us and control us to keep them on top.

But our troops will storm their Headquarters and put this genocide to a stop.

The creator of evil-Satan is mad because we will take down his earthly hell.
Babylon will fall and the fires will lick its skin; your plan has failed.
Don't pray to God now, it's too late.
There is no redemption-500 years ago, you have sealed your fate.
Bathe in your poison and the fires of your soul.
This revolution, you cannot control.
God has flooded the skies with our blood as the souls of our ancestors come out of the trees.
Fire has come to consume your lives as you scream for a cup of water or a cool breeze.
It is time to pay the price of your sins as you feel the fire.
We will haunt you in your nightmares; psychological, mental and physical torture rises higher.
You think that you're prepared for world war 3, but this is not a war.
As we feel your wicked wind blow through our hoods, this is something that you cannot prepare for.

As you feel your soul burning and your so called nation falling to the ground.
You collapse and look up to the red skies and scream "what have I done all around?"
You just wait until your body completely burns and your black soul goes up to God to be judged.
Praying and crying to spare you from hell.
Your blood boils and smoke you smell.

It's Time for Afrikans to Rise Up

Stand up and break those chains!
As the patrols keep watch; it's time to let the fires of our 400 years of our slavery reign.
Slavery and colonialism no more, Afrika will retaliate.
This is a warning that her soldiers on the way; we won't stop, it's too late.
The world as we know it will end; Babylon will die.
The European Global Power Structure will burn in flames and we will laugh as we watch them cry.
Watch as the American flag bleeds.
Capitalism, imperialism, neo-colonialism are the offspring of its venomous seeds.

Stand up and break those chains!
Watch them run in fear as we rise; they think that we're insane.
Gods and Goddesses; let's rise my Afrikan Kings and Queens.
No matter where we live and our differences, it's time to march for the Red, Black and Green.
I'm done kissing their asses like I'm their nigger.
Like some docile house pet to make their pockets bigger.
Love and unity-no more are we bitches and hoes.
Real niggas turning into real men; they will reap what they sow.

Huey P. Newton Jr. got the military importing us guns
screaming "Afrikan liberation and Black Power!"
I thought it was over until John Henrik Clarke, Amos
Wilson, Claud Anderson, Dr. Yosef Ben walked in
giving us knowledge to uplift, build, unify and empower.

Stand up and break those chains!
Drake said it best, our worst behavior; it's time to show
what runs in our veins.
They never loved us and they never will.
They live in their fantasy land while they steal, lie,
exploit, destroy and kill.
The gunshot heard around the world; they aren't
prepared for what's coming ahead.
They think Baltimore is something, watch as all of their
negropeans, coons, puppets and Charles Barkleys
mysteriously show up dead.
The lord is crying for them, the Bible warned them to be
prepared.
Afrika isn't playing anymore; we're glad they're scared.
Nation building as we employ our people in our own
stores.
Our black owned schools with Afrikan Centered
Education open up their doors.
RBG flags fly all through the air as fire licks that red
white and blue.

Stand up and break those chains!
Mental, physical, economic, political and social
revolution is what we will gain.
If they mess with one of us; they mess with all the
Afrikan Kings.

The souls of Dr. Khalid Muhammed and Nat Turner are resurrected as the slave bell rings.
Let's go find Mr. Lynch and put that whip on his back.
Let's see how many bull whips make him crack.
What FBI, what CIA?
They've already been infiltrated, taken down; I thought I told them that we don't play.
Are they going to try to send the military to exterminate all Afrikans in America and in Afrika, an entire continent?
If they step on our RBG flag, arrest them because that's what we represent.

Stand up and break those chains!
Whoever conquers the mind controls the body, but now we control our brains.
We have Afrikan Psych and Self-Knowledge classes rolling with Adisa Franklin, Joy Angela Degruy, Ra Un Nefer Amen and Dr. Na'im Akbar.
It's time to accept our divinity as we call on our ancestors to open our eyes to our power from the sun, the moon and the stars.
Stand up and break those chains to gain knowledge of self, love of self, discipline and control of self.
Knowledge of our people, love of our people, respect of our people and Afrikan/black UNITY.
We are one people, one continent, one love and one community.
Reviving Marcus Garvey and Malcolm X.
Our brains are going on knowledge overload; watch those Afrikans flex.

Kwame Nkrumah and Kwame Touré rise from their graves.
Even Martin Luther King wants a piece of the action; we got him ready to misbehave.

Stand up and break those chains!
They don't understand our humiliation, struggle, torture and pain.
Afrika uniting and accepting their Afrikan brothers and sisters in the diaspora.
Our mother refuses to keep getting raped and stolen from; our resurrected Mother Afrika.
During Afrikan and Native slavery, they cut off hands, our mother is about to start cutting dicks.
Her vagina and her legs are closed to thieves and their bag of tricks.
I guess the world really is coming to an end as we have all of our resurrected Afrikan teachers and leaders standing by our side.
It's time to stand up and break those chains; it's time to teach, heal, lead, revolutionize, and ride.

Burn The Babylon Slave Plantations!

Burn!
Babylon burn!
It's time to fuck shit up and burn shit down.
I see these skyscrapers that don't belong to me, so it's time to burn it to the ground.
Burn this shitty U.S money.
Burn this whole muthafuckin country.
They think that I'm a terrorist, let's see if I am when they're sitting there dead.
Major corporations in flames.
Pouring gasoline like a mentally ill white boy.
Black bullets flying but it's only a decoy.
We screaming fuck the White House while we blowing that shit up.
What CIA, what FBI? It's time to shut their asses up.

All of our shit belongs to the bank.
Europeans own our shit; we are their slaves as we sit in their military tank.
We fight to protect their rights, their interests and their money.
We think that we are balling, bad bitches, real niggas; we think that it's funny.
We don't own McDonalds but they are selling us poison right in our faces.

We salute an American flag that created slaves and
genocide of other races.
We spend their money in their stores.
We say fuck them but we send our children in their
school house doors.
That nice car you have is theirs.
They force us to pay taxes for their spending affairs.
We work in their million dollar corporations while barely
making minimum wage.
Barely able to survive because of their greediness; we're
slaves of the new age.
If we break the law, we rot in prison, but I guess it's an
upgrade.
They break the law and kill millions of people but get
paid.

You looking fly in their name brand shoes, purses, make
up and clothes.
We are their slaves, their bitches and hoes.
We fight over their hoods and their materialistic shit.
We want the newest name brands but can't pay the JEA
bill for their house, we still buy it.
We use their guns.
We kill each other for their things and think it's fun.
We use and sell their drugs.
They say that we are real niggas now but we are just
their slave-puppet thugs.
They own our education, our jobs and our lives.
We live by what they tell us, we believe whatever they
tell us even though it's lies.
They throw us in their prisons and jails.
We are new age slaves in their Babylon hell.

What do we own-a street corner, a hood?
Do we even own our own food?
Who owns the planes, cars, businesses and guns?
While we banging on each other because of the hood we "own", they're killing us for fun.
Who imports the drugs in our hood, who writes the history and science books?
Who grows the GMO foods that we eat and cook?
Who tells us to be nonviolent while they go to war with the rest of the world, kill us like animals and commit holocausts and genocides?
Who controls your paycheck from which you provide?
Who controls the media, T.V and radio stations, and the news?
Who indoctrinated and brainwashed you into believing everything they tell you?
Who controls the schools and the white-washed, indoctrinated, European based, systematic brainwashing, corporate-controlled education system?
Who owns the International Monetary Fund and the World Bank, the United Nations, the Department of Defense and capitalism?
Who created and controls exploitation, Africom, Planned Parenthood, imperialism, and neo-colonialism?
Who created and controls the Prison Industrial Complex, the CIA and FBI, the pharmaceutical industry?
Who started the World Health Organization, the theft, control and exploitation of the music industry?
Who owns the military and tells us to fight and kill for their greedy and selfish interests in the name of American democracy?

Who do we steal resources and slaughter innocent
people for just for them to claim there's no such thing as
white supremacy?
Who told you to say the pledge of allegiance and salute
their bloody flag while falling for their tricks?
Who told us to vote democrat and republican that they
control; who told us to believe in their politricks?
Who tells us that we are African American or just
American?
Who tells us that Africa is home of black apes who live
in trees and we aren't Afrikan?
Who tells us that Jesus is European-white?
Who told us to just sit, pray and wait on white Jesus to
save us instead of getting up to fight?

Fuck their money, greed, power and control.
Fuck their European Global Power Structure and their
corrupted ass voting polls.
Fuck their European cracka Jesus.
Fuck a damn white Christmas.
Fuck their law.
Fuck their big ass houses as we tearing it down with
chain saws.
Fuck their slave catchers-the crooked ass cops.
Fuck their military; it's all about to stop.
Fuck their white-washed, indoctrinated, European based,
systematic brainwashing, corporate-controlled education
system.
Fuck their theft, control and exploitation of the music
industry into their slave market system.
Fuck their hoes, bitches and coons.
It's time to burn and slaughter all of that shit.

"The price of freedom is death"-Malcolm X; they will threaten us with jail and death but we can't quit.

Burn that American flag, watch they asses cry.
We're laughing as we throw up RBG flags; white supremacy shall die.
The motherfuckas calling the military.
But they can't get rid of the RBG gang-the Afrikan community.
Black guerillas taking over the Department of Defense while we link up with our Native Americans to create our own military.
I see them slave catchers cops trying to throw us in jail.
I'm a runaway slave trying to burn down this Babylon hell.
Malcolm X and Marcus Garvey runs through my veins.
Huey P Newton and Nat Turner are in my head while Brother Khalid Muhammed telling me to make it rain.

Coons and negopeans mysteriously show up dead.
Snitches and slave master lovers will get two shots in the head.
Martin Luther King pacifists telling me to forgive and just pray.
White Jesus lovers telling me to sit down and wait to Jesus comes to save us and turn gay.
Sit and turn gay while Europeans stick their white dick up my ass.
Letting them rape me and my family and get rid of us fast.
Shooting and killing us like helpless monkeys while calling us nigger animals.

Feeding us to sharks and dogs; who are the real cannibals?
So fuck the white Jesus lovers and Martin Luther King pacifists too.
This is over 400 years of nasty Afrikan and Native American stew.

Retaliation? No, it's just our justice.
Reparations in blood and fire.
Burn the slave plantations and watch as the smoke rise higher.
They are fucking with the wrong Afrikan, the new age rebellious field slave.
It's time to make them feel what hell feels like as I put Babylon in its grave.

The United "Snakes" States of America-The Great Red, White and Blue: In the "White" God We Trust!

Red is the blood of our Afrikan and Native American ancestors that built this nation.
Red is the hatred and discrimination.
Red is the smell of death and our blood flowing from our bodies on the trees.
Red is the blood splattered when they whipped us whenever they please.
Red is the blood shed when we go to war.
Red is the blood of our people dying to oil, power and money and having the people tell you of the death at your door.
Red is my history erased through brainwashing, torture, pain and lies.
Red is the ignored screams and cries.
Red is my Afrikan brothers and sisters in the hood and the streets who're struggling.

Red is my Afrikan brothers and sisters that are being set up in the "white" system while hustling.
Red is my mother who has a Masters Degree but can't find a job to put food on the table.
Red is my Afrikan brother working hard to get in college and make able.
Red is "No Justice, No Peace".
Red is the gunfire of Europeans that is supposed to protect us and make all problems cease.
Red is my brothers and sisters gunned down in the street.
Red is the struggle of this oppressive system that we're constantly trying to beat.
Red is the label and treatment that we get just for being black.
Red is the target that we will always have on our backs.

White signifies the White European Global Power Structure.
White is the eradication of the Afrikan and Native American culture.
White is the European mindset that they are clean and pure.
White is the master color, European is the master race, stealing and stripping Afrika of her future.
White is the American dream, the American pride.
White is the color in which you can get away with murder.
White is the color in which cops can kill innocent people while their children scream "don't hurt her".
White is the color in which you are above the law.
White is the color that beat us Afrikans skin raw.
White is the Constitution for them and by them.

White is “God” and everyone must bow down to “him”.
White is power, money and status, but they forgot to tell you that it also means greed.
White means dominant power over every piece of land and race of people around the earth; more than they need.
While is murder justified by self-defense or mental illness.
White is without sin and imperfections-silent stillness.

Blue is the lies implanted in our minds.
Blue is the brainwashing of the Afrikan kind.
Blue is the lies taught to our children from elementary to high school.
Blue is the flawed constitution, government and unsaid rules.
Blue are the Negropeans put in place to keep the Afrikan Nation from rising.
Blue is the “we are all Afrikan/human” excuse to stay on top of us and stop us from surviving.
Blue is the virus experiments implanted in our blood.
Blue is the drug system that is pushed and used in the hood.
Blue is the jail cells being filled up with Afrikans doing good.
Blue is freedom and rights that we are supposed to have from this slave fueled government.
Blue is the protection that we’re supposed to have from the corrupted police and the military that was sent.
Blue is the unseen racism and labels that we get with our so called equality.

Blue is the false hope from president Obama, any
president and any European political party.

The stars is world domination.
The stars signifies owning the heaven and all the planets.
The stars signifies owning all the people and resources in
the world.
The stars mean that they have a divine right to rule over
everything and everyone.

Red, White and Blue-The great U.S.A.
The United States of death, lies, guns, power and slaves,
but we salute the flag every day.
The United States of Europe that stripped us of our
Afrikan and Native American culture.
The United States that brainwashed our future.
The United States of the European Global Power
Structure.
The United States that tortured, killed and raped our
women.
The United States that whipped, killed and mated our
men.
The United States thinks of us as animals and locks us
up in cages.
The United States that plaster God as their faces.

In the White God We Trust-Are we the modern day
Sodom and Gomorrah; will this nation be struck down in
Hell?
Founded upon religious men with morals and
principles-no one can tell.

Is this your United States of America?
I swear my allegiance to the United Nation of Afrika.

Is this your corrupted Red, White and Blue?
Is this your slave fueled United States of America?
Is this your tainted and torn flag?
Is this your "his" "story" laced with lies and wrapped in tattered rags?

The great "White God" bless the great corrupted United Snakes-I mean, "United States of America"!
In Guns, Lies, Power, Money, Greed, Indoctrination and Racism We Trust!

Mon(K)ey

Mon(k)ey
Money or monkey?
Which one is the key?
They think of us as one and the other is all that we can see.
As we scream racism, cops, knowledge is a mystery.
We are taught that we were slaves but don't understand the psychological slavery.
Can money buy our happiness or can it buy our freedom?
What they don't teach us is that they control our minds to stay slaves and be dumb.
No more fuck the cops, white people and the government is the reason.
We don't even understand what we are doing-committing psychological and racial treason.

Bitch, you better have my money.
What's in it for me, how much money?
I don't care about anything except my money.
I'm on that paper chase-I'm chasing that money.
Fuck unity-I'm unified to my money.
I don't know myself-I know money.
I have no self-knowledge-I just have money.
I don't love myself-I just love money.
I don't care about history-I only care about my money.

Vote? I'm going to vote for whoever gives me the most money.
Family? My family is my money.
All these bitches want is money.
All these niggas want is money.
God-who is God? GOD IS MONEY!

While they come into our hoods, shooting us to the ground while screaming "monkey niggers die!".
All we do is complain, only if it messes up our money-then we cry.
We don't mind if they call us a monkey…
As long as we receive that money.
Which one is the key?
Completely lose all sanity and say forget our history?
While they label us, call us whatever they want, treat us however they please just for some money.
Then what do we do with that money- give it back to them- place it back in their hands?
Buy their European brand clothes, shoes, bags without investing in our black owned stores, restaurants, clothes, banks-when will we understand?

Monkey-put them on a chain-tell them that they are savages and we are their savior- they will obey.
They will teach their youth to do what we tell them, pray to us and believe anything we say.
Monkey-give them just enough where they won't complain.
They give us free food, free healthcare, free stuff and a black president but no economic or political power or gain.

We send our children to their public school as they
brainwash and indoctrinate our youth with their lies.
They tell us to vote either democrat or republican and if
our party doesn't win- we go up in cries.
They tell us equality and post-racial Amerikkka because
racism doesn't exist anymore and we believe.
They tell us to pay them for college lies just to graduate
and work for them 9 to 5 minimum wage and we
believe.
We are their street soldiers as we kill our own and infect
each other with their poisonous drug game.
We would sell out our own people and our hoods just for
their money and fame.
They poison our food and we eat it.
While they claim that fruit and salad is healthy-they
inject growth hormones in our animals and all of that
shit.
We will be happy and content with whatever we see.
we will call it progress and leave them be.
While they brainwash and indoctrinate our youth in their
12-year brainwashing camp.
Then exploit the brainwashed through their college lies
that we pay for-giving us their corporate America stamp.
College too expensive-join their military.
They will have us kill our own and other innocent lives
just because they are money hungry and resource greedy.

Money or Monkey?
Which one is the key?
We call our own stupid when they try to teach us about
nation building and unity.

We ignore our ancestors that laid the foundations such as Malcolm X, Kwame Nkrumah, Kwame Touré (Stokely Carmichael), John Henrik Clarke, Dr. Amos Wilson, Claud Anderson, Dr Yosef Ben Jochannan, Adisa Franklin and Marcus Garvey.
Instead we would rather be content with complaining and wait on someone else to change.
We don't want to change ourselves so we just blame everything on the government and say that that's how it is arranged.
The plight of our Afrikan race is alive and well because we are brain dead.
A generational mentality that the white man is our savior and we must believe anything that is spoon fed.
When will we wake up and see what is right in front of our faces?

It's like Satan giving a gift to God.
Tricking him to go against everything good-turning him into a fraud.
Satan then saying that he could help- God he can save.
Reversing everything created where Satan is God and God is Satan and God is now his slave.

What Lies Between Your Life, Mind and Emotions

Intoxicated memories create blackholes of impurity.
Allowing suicide to flood by your own insecurity.
Your sins intimidate your mind to gulp down your brain cells.
They burrow holes and make homes in your emptiness to make you fail.
Viruses open their sticky hands to take hold of your mind.
Breaking down your foundation while implanting pains to remind.
Prying your fingers off of your only existence of sanity.
Replacing reality with fantasy.

As you crawl, trying to rise, you find that none of this makes any sense.
Blood boiling, brain intoxicated, body failing, not knowing whether it's the past, present or future tense.
Where's the medicine man?
Why can't you understand?
Blood trickling down.
Tears sprinting towards the ground.
Silent screams frantically trying to crawl out of your throat.

Suicide notes tainted with knife wounds.

Homicidal feet tramping on your heart.
Vindictive hands plucking your feeble body apart.
They are trying to take control and force you with hurt and lies.
They will make you think that death is pleasure to silence your cries.

Close your eyes.
Delve into your thoughts until you realize.
Let your best thoughts and memories drown you into another existence.
Tell everyone who you are and what you are feeling, poetry is your resistance.
Allow your skin to open and your flesh to show.
Choke your veins to kill death and let your blood flow.
Take that gun down; it is not time for you to die
Let your fingers scream and allow your pen to cry.

Write until you feel no more.
Let the thoughts flow until your fingers are bloody and sore.
Show the world what you are feeling by breathing your emotions through written words.
This is your poem, do whatever you want with it.
It is time for you to take control and make sure that no one forgets it.
I am officially done with my part as I give you the paper and the pen.

It is time for you to grab hold of them, let your heart bleed, open your mind and let the words flow from within.

Keep Writing

Keep writing
Let the pens go up in flames
I don't care what is going on in your life; let everyone know your name.

Keep writing
Don't be deceived by what man tells you.
Stay strong regardless of what you are going through.

Keep writing
Unleash your anger, fears and hate.
Bleed out all of your emotions and start a clean slate.

Keep writing
Poetry is our only existence.
It is our lives, our power, our fire, our insurgency, and our resistance.

Keep writing
Don't stop until you're throwing balls of fire.
Unleashing it from your pen, pencil and mouth to let poetry rise higher.

Keep writing
Poetry is our insurgency.
We will soon reach full capacity.
Our words are the bombs and we are the terrorists.

We have field men, airmen, ship-men, flamethrowers
and arsonists.

Keep writing
Let poetry rise from the east to the west.
It is time to wake up all of the poets in the world and put
them to the test.

Keep writing
Put down that knife from cutting yourself; throw away
your thoughts of suicide.
Pick up your pens, pencils, paper and microphones and
slaughter the world with your power, which they tried to
make you hide.

Keep writing
Put down that make up and look at your pretty face.
Quit those diets and look how good your body looks;
show people how poetry looks and tastes.

Keep writing
If you're lonely and have no friends, allow poetry to
warm your soul and be your best friend.
Just start writing and poetry will put you in another land.

Keep writing
Forget about those people who keep spreading rumors,
lies and stereotypes.
Drop lyrical bombs on them; beat them with your poetic
whip to leave them with lacerations and stripes.

Keep writing

Never stop, never give up and never let your opponent win.
If you need help, you have billions of poets across the globe to help you with the war within.

Keep writing
It is time to revolutionize.
We are the chosen ones and we must make people realize.
You might be the black sheep, the misfit, the outcast, but you must let poetry open up your enemy's eyes.
Let it flow out of you, exposing your emotions, the truth and their lies.

Just keep writing
Stop crying but let the pen cry your tears.
All poets will rise; your time is very near.
We're waiting for you to help us revolutionize by poetry and getting poets to unite.
Don't put down that pen, pencil or microphone, keep the poetic fight.

Just keep writing
Regardless if you're rich, poor, old, young, in trouble, homeless or in stress.
As long as you hold on to your pen, pencil or microphone, your poetry will do the rest.

Chains to Change from the Art in Our Veins

Where are we? Lost in our own ignorance and exasperation.
Dead in our history while basking in our "more" generation.
Faltering in our steps and swimming in our failures by lack of education.
Taking what we think we know while wanting more materialistic sensations.
The belief in super imposed lies.
The color lines exploited to cause more cries.
Insecurity nibbling on our veins, slowly stealing our sanity.
Existence running into the lines of fantasy and reality.
Rust and mold grows on our skin.
Allowing inhibitions to take over by seeping sins.

It is time to rise from our ignorance and failures by art and dreams.
Fear and ignorance strangles our masculinity while our morals hang by the seams.
I grab the keys to unlock our souls from the new age slavery.
Trying to uncuff us from the struggle of reality.
Our blood flows through our family's star crossed tears and pains.

Our hatred, violence and mentality allows myonecrosis
to flow through our broken veins.
We rot out the good by evil and hate in the hearts
construction.
We are predators of ourselves and victims of our
self-created life of destruction.
Repeating the history of our ancestors to bound us in this
condition of psychosis.
We've stopped fighting throughout history as our souls
are raped by sin and darkness.

The cells in my mind are raped by the roaring fire in my
heaving chest.
While my tongue and lungs are raw from silent screams,
there's no time to rest.
My ravenous rotting fingers grow teeth as my hands pick
up the pen to write.
There's no time to wait, I have to fight.
Knowing and going through the struggle.
I look through my mentality of self- concealment to
decompress our emotions through our blood puddles.

The sharp edge of silence slices my throat; forcing my
suppressed words of emotion to breathe.
Allowing my raging spirit to rise in resilience.
My thoughts flow through the battle zone of experience
laced with my creativity.
Thinking of ways to break down concrete jungles with
dreams; artistically.
To be able to drink out of used grenades and build homes
out of abandoned military tanks.

My screams echo off of the jelly filled walls of my
conscious banks.
The tyrant inside of me screams the anthem of
revolution.
I shake hands with thugs, artists and poets while we draft
the new world order solution.
It is time to rise, conquer and change.
Stand up from being a slave and change.
Unify with art and poetry and change.
It is time to take back our souls, our nation and our
world.

The Poetic War

I have risen; walking out of the cemetery, coming from the graves.
I am the leader of the poetic insurgents; my masses come in waves.
It is time for someone to stand up and revolutionize.
The Artistic Revolution and the Poetry Movement is what we must realize.
We use lyricism to influence minds and use what we have in our hands, mouths and minds to fight.
Some of us have writing syndrome and will write all night.

We write, we think, we speak and we will win; victory we will find.
We open up minds as people read and listen to the words blasting in their mind.
Poetry is our principal but non-violence is only a tactic; the people shall choose.
If we have to kill people or severely injure them, we will do whatever it takes and use whatever we need to use.

We use internal rhyme to force people to comprehend the hidden messages within the lines.
We use no rhyme and start using prose with a new surprise every time.
Intertwining messages to let art be expressed by didactics.

Using satiric poetry as a tactic.
Mixing it to be highly dangerous, confronting and provocative with multiple human wave attacks.
Dropping high explosive incendiary shrapnel in your brain like we are in Iraq.
Our ink blots fly faster and paralyze people to make them sit and stare.
Our pens; some are M-46s, some are M-3s and others are MAT-49s, ready to shoot down anyone who says that they don't care.

Artists start coming together with poets to break the creative barrier between them and take the people by surprise.
We use decapitation and vivisection to cut off the blood flow of the human brain by our artistic ties.
We infect like bacteria and viruses; some of us using euphony and some of us are using rhyme.
We will have electricity running through your veins like you're reading a terrorist plan crime.

Trapping people in history as we use allusion.
Then shoot them in a metaphorical world of life's illusion.
We leave people lost and feeble in perpetual darkness.
Where a vast expression of nothingness surrounds people's senses.
We tell them to close their eyes and feel.
Sense and feel the emotions we write that are real.
People have lost their sense of emotion and touch and let their eyesight judge.

Forgetting about feelings, but we will turn their heart back to a human from the grudge.
We use tactical ambushes with the microphone as we slaughter people with spoken word.
Letting our emotions fly like birds.
We are like the Nazi storm troopers who stood around the Opera House chanting "Full powers or else! We want the Bill or fire and murder."
We want people to read, feel and understand that poetry is life and we will die for it as martyrs.
We don't need strict security; we just let our minds flow.
We unleash our words out of our mouths and let our tongues go.
Our hands write like cars on I-95.
Going 80 miles an hour, wrecking everyone because we don't care how we drive.

It is time to fight and show our true qualities and emotions.
We will show people why we write poetry and what poetry is as we set the pages ablaze and run it in motion.
We want to help the world but the eyes of the poet are what they don't understand.
We are the new world; soon, the Poetry Movement will sweep across the land.
Defeat and retreat is impossible with our mouths to speak and our hands of slaughter.
Using our innovative, productive and prodigious tactics, we never falter.
Ambitious, dedicated and determined poets take on leading us into the war.

We enhance and grow our skills from learning
information and ideas from each other to let our
creativity soar.

We let poetry seep into the streets where the thugs drop
their guns and drugs and start killing and selling pens
and paper.
The child molesters forget about abducting children and
start writing about how he really doesn't want to rape
her.
As rival gang member lyricists and metaphorical minds
come together.
We shake hands and form the poetic bond that can't be
bent or broken forever.
Thugs and lawyers come together with one common
goal: write, speak and fight.
Gaining new perspectives and learning about issues
facing our communities and our nation.
Different races coming together in one congregation.
Democrats and republicans forget about politics and start
to look through the poets eyes.
We inject Marxism with chlorine gas so our objective is
not a disguise.

This is not communism; don't always believe what you
hear.
We are just trying to get the nations eyes; so come fight
with us or die in fear.
The constitution can't keep us under control; we rain
trench mortars and lay siege to the White House.

The Bill of Rights doesn't give us our true freedom and independence; will the president give in and retreat, or even his spouse?

Poetry and art fused together with spoken word by lawyers, jail men, congressmen, thugs and ordinary people like me.
We will fight until we gain access to everyone's poetic eyes.
We will die fighting and our grandchildren will fight until we reach the ultimate prize.
One day, this movement will stretch across planet earth.
The Poetry Movement, that's been going on before my birth.

Use Me

If you can't stop hurting, then I can't wait.
If you want to die, then you are my fate.
If you want to stop breathing, then kill me too.
If you can't go anymore, I'll pull you through.
If you don't want to feel anymore, give me your pain.
If you just want out, then make me insane.
If you can't see the light, let me be your glasses.
Obviously, you're blind. If you feel low, let me feel up
your glass.

If you feel manipulated, then use me.
Let me be your pillow you cry on, your wall you beat
on-I want you to abuse me.
If you feel like going off, then curse me out.
Let me be your rag doll; tear my flesh out.
If you want to throw something, throw me around.
Bust my head onto the ground.
If you want to do something stupid and insane, fuck me
until I can't fuck anymore.
If you want to get back all the fuckboys, cut off my dick
and leave it bloody at my door.
Be my personal vampire-bite me.
Suck all my blood and turn me.
Drink all of it, take my soul and heart.
Take whatever you want and shred it apart.
If you want to take drugs, I want you to be my drug-my
crack/cocaine.

Addicted to your love-hate-abusive relationship; make me go insane.
I love it!
I'll love you for it.
Fuck me up for every fuckboy and fake friend in your life.
Slap the fuck out of my face.
Play with my body until it's a disgrace.
Strangle me until I give you my last breath.
As long as you're alive, safe and happy with no more pain and anger- I'll die a happy death.
Pour your heart onto my feeble flesh.
Whip me until my blood is fresh.
I will forgive you-I'm your ride or die.
Let's fuck up the world; as we laugh, they cry.
Shooting at the hating, backstabbing, lying mothafuckas.
You're laughing and speechless but this ain't no mothafucking game.
I want your inner craziness, your pain, fears, your hatred-I'm tired of the same ol same.
Let's fly away and start over.
Or you can just fuck me up and when you've had enough, run me over.
Let's go psycho…
You already think I am, you probably are too-so let's go.

Deeper

I want to go deeper with her.
Deeper than the ocean-positive energy transfer.
Brain explosions from going too deep.
Psychologically in-sync through paradoxical sleep.
Deeper than the benthic zone.
I want to get to know the marrow of your bone.
Keep your body, I want your heart, mind and soul.
Let's go so deep, we break social control.
So deep we find mental, spiritual and economic freedom.
It's time to break our "free"dome.
I want her to go so deep that she becomes my Goddess!

I want to go so deep that she puts her pussy on my plate.
Juices flowing out while I'm eating my steak.
So deep that I fuck her brain.
Making love to her mind while knowledge overload
makes her go insane.
So deep that she feels no pain or fear.
So deep that when I'm gone, her mind I'm here.
So deep I conquered the deepest part of her fantasy.
So deep that we both forgot what was reality.
Let's go crazy deep-deeper than our wildest dreams.
I want to hear singing when she screams.
I want to go so deep we forget about time.
So deep that going too deep was a crime.
So deep that when we're mad-we laugh and pillow fight.

Fuck bouncing that ass, let's have mind blowing conversations all night.
I want to go so deep, past the g-spot.
She won't even be able to scream stop.
So deep that our love is insane.
Loyal as fuck and no cheating game.

I want to go so deep that I can say, fuck pussy and ass.
I just want to kiss her and our relationship lasts.
Where I love you means something more than fucking you at night.
I want to cook you food while you talk about your day.
I want to go so deep that just looking at you takes my breath away.
I want a deep ass relation but no ship.
Because ships sink and I don't need that shit.

www.ingramcontent.com/pod-product-compliance
Lightning Source LLC
Chambersburg PA
CBHW051733130826
49812CB00033B/845

9789357445382